CHRISTAS
— *IS A PROMISE* —

JONI EARECKSON TADA

Rummaging through our garage one December afternoon, I sniffed the unmistakable fragrance of new leather. My seven-year-old fingers found it behind a box—a new pony bridle.

From that very moment, Santa Claus was dethroned from my childhood. No more leaving milk and cookies on the mantelpiece on Christmas Eve. No more pleading letters to the North Pole. No more sugar and carrots for the reindeer. I was relieved. Something deep down had told me that it was all a ploy, anyway.

From then on, December 25th carried a new meaning. It was a special day—a holy day. The candlelight service on Christmas Eve at church had a new and deeper meaning. Almost overnight, Christmas Eve became one of those "silent nights" to ponder the miracle of Jesus.

And ponder I did, long and earnest. But always, as I sat back into the pew, I expected something else to happen—something to fill the longing inside of me. I know now that I was deep into a Christmas longing. It's a longing each of us senses this time of year—especially when we listen to the child inside of us. It's a desire to be home, to belong, to find fulfillment, complete and eternal. Christmas is an invitation to a celebration yet to happen.

On this side of eternity, Christmas is a promise. The Savior brings inner peace to those who receive him. But the story is not finished until there is peace in our world.

Every Christmas is still a "turning of the page" until Jesus returns. Every December 25th marks another year that draws us closer to the fulfillment of the ages, that draws us closer to our heavenly home. Every Christmas carol is a beautiful echo of the heavenly choir that will one day fill the universe with joy and singing. Each Christmas gift is a foreshadowing of the gifts of golden crowns to be cast at the feet of the King of Kings.

Each smile, each embrace, beckons us onward and calls us upward when those who have received the gift of God's Son will see the Lord face to face.

Angels hovering over treetops may have heralded his birth in the Bethlehem night, but one day they will herald the dawning of a new day.

This Christmas I pray that God will fill the longing of your heart with the reality of his Son. May the babe of Bethlehem who gave his life on the cross of Calvary bring you love and joy and peace throughout the year and on into eternity.

> *"...behold, I bring you good news of great joy that will be for all the people. For unto you is born this day in the city of David a Savior, who is Christ the Lord."*

Luke 2:10–11

CROSSWAY | GOOD NEWS Tracts

ISBN 978-1-68216-344-3

www.goodnewstracts.org